Basketball Legends

Activity Wizo

Please consider writing a review!

Just visit: activitywizo.com/review

Copyright 2020. Activity Wizo.

All Rights Reserved.

No part of this book may be reproduced or transmitted

in any form or by any means, electronic or mechanical, including

photocopying, recording or by any other form without written

permission from the publisher.

Have questions? We want to hear from you!

Email us at: support@activitywizo.com

ISBN: 978-1-951806-24-8

FREE BONUS

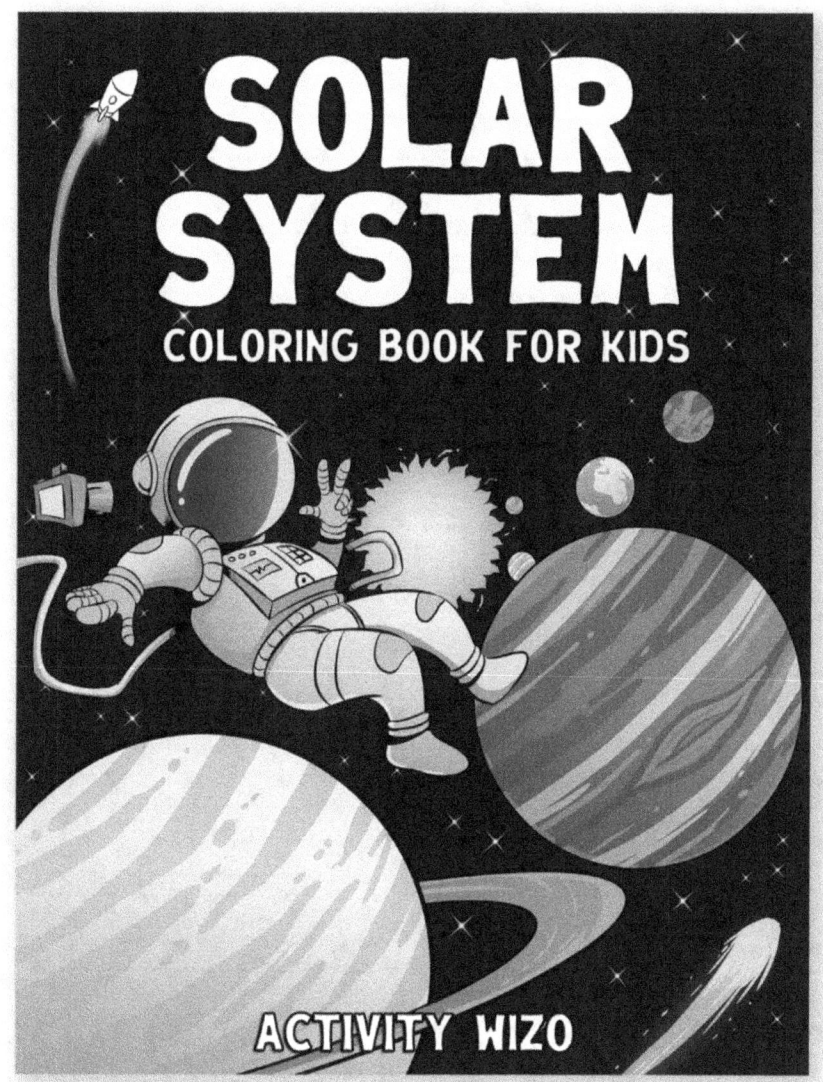

Get This FREE Bonus Now!

Just go to: activitywizo.com/free

Table of Contents

Charles Barkley 6

Chris Paul 8

David Robinson 10

Dennis Rodman 12

Dirk Nowitzki 14

Dwyane Wade 16

Giannis Antetokounmpo 18

Isiah Thomas 20

James Harden 22

Jason Kidd 24

John Stockton 26

Kareem Abdul-Jabbar 28

Karl Malone 30

Kawhi Leonard 32

Kevin Durant 34

Kevin Garnett 36

Klay Thompson 38

Kobe Bryant 40

Kyrie Irving 42

Larry Bird 44

LeBron James 46

Magic Johnson 48

Manu Ginobili 50

Michael Jordan 52

Patrick Ewing 54

Paul Pierce 56

Reggie Miller 58

Russell Westbrook 60

Scottie Pippen 62

Shaquille O'Neal 64

Stephen Curry 66

Steve Nash 68

Tim Duncan 70

Tony Parker 72

Vince Carter 74

Yao Ming 76

Allen Iverson 78

Anthony Davis 80

Ben Wallace 82

Blake Griffin 84

Charles Barkley

The man with too many nicknames to count, Charles Barkley, was one of the best never to win it all. An undersized big man who used his wide girth to gobble up all of the rebounds. Barkley grabbed more than 10 rebounds per game in 15 of 16 seasons, and this earned him the name, 'the Round Mound of Rebound.' Though he was celebrated on the court, Barkley certainly had haters throughout his career with multiple fights on and off-court along with an infamous spitting incident, which left him as a divisive figure.

Barkley was drafted as a junior with the 5th pick of the 1984 Draft by the Philadelphia 76ers. His play with them proved that he would go on to be one of the best forwards in the mid-80s. Out of the eight years he played in Philadelphia, the team went on to reach the playoffs six times. During these playoffs, he averaged 22.4 points and 13.1 rebounds per game while shooting at 67%. Following a disappointing season in 1991-92, Barkley was sold to Phoenix, where his impact was felt immediately.

He led the Suns to a league-best of 62 wins, where he won the league's MVP. His regular-season play never brought him a championship though, as the Chicago Bulls defeated Barkley's Suns in six games, which was the only championship he played in. He played three more seasons in Phoenix and was sold to Houston, where he finished his career.

An 11-time All-Star, Charles Barkley, retired in 2000 and became the fourth player ever to have over 20,000 points, 10,000 rebounds, and 4,000 assists in his career. Following his career, Charles Barkley perhaps gained his most fame on television as a studio analyst.

Chris Paul

A defensive stalwart and true floor general, Chris Paul has been one of the premier point guards of the NBA since his debut. Drafted fourth overall in 2005 out of Wake Forest University, Paul began his career with New Orleans. He was the winner of the 2006 Rookie of the Year Award but missed on being selected unanimously by a single vote.

In 2007, Paul earned his first All-Star nomination and was selected to the All-Defensive team. That was just the tip of the iceberg in his breakout season, as he was voted second in the MVP race.

After the 2010 season, Paul was involved in a trade controversy with New Orleans and the two Los Angeles teams. The league voided the trade to the Lakers, and Paul eventually landed with the Clippers. There, Paul teamed up with Blake Griffin and DeAndre Jordan to form "Lob City," a team that was known for alley-oops and high-flying dunks. His time in Los Angeles saw Paul reach the playoffs six times, but he never reached the NBA Finals.

The Houston Rockets traded for Paul following the 2017 season, and he went on to help the team to win a franchise-record 65 games in his debut season. He also came closest to reaching the finals in 2018, losing back-to-back games to Golden State in the Conference Finals. Following the 2019 season, Paul was again traded, this time to Oklahoma City. Off the court, Chris Paul is most famous for his State Farm commercials, along with serving as the NBA Players Association's President.

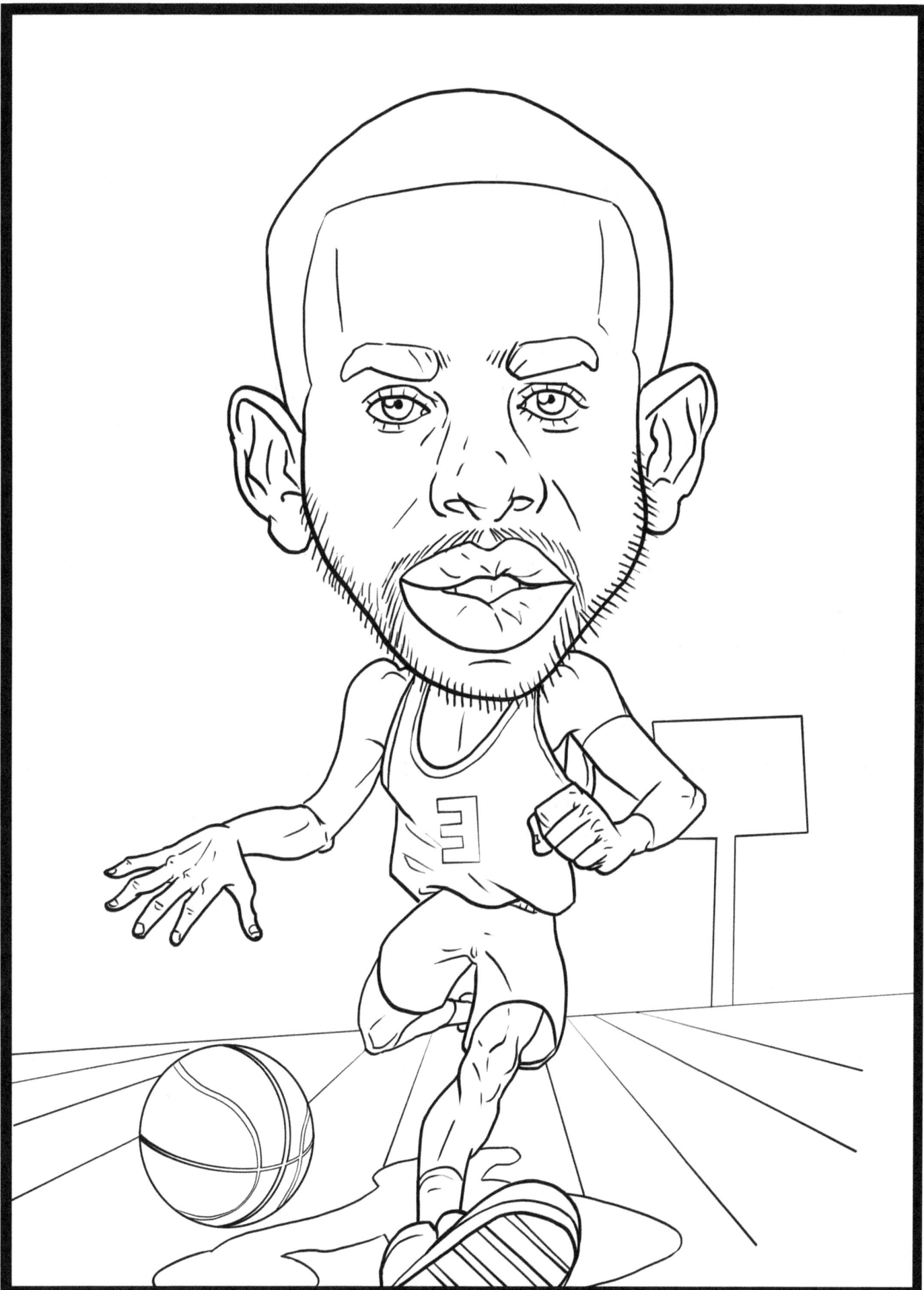

David Robinson

Known simply as "The Admiral," David Robinson led the initial charge for the beginning of the Spurs dynasty and transformed himself into an all-time great player. Prior to attending the Naval Academy, Robinson had only played organized basketball as a 6'6" senior in high school. By the time he finished his collegiate career, Robinson had grown to 7'0". Before signing with the San Antonio Spurs, Robinson served at a naval base in Georgia to fulfill his service requirements.

During his first season in the league, Robinson average over 24 points, 12 rebounds, and almost four blocks per game. With those statistics in hand, Robinson was named the best rookie in the league in 1990. The first seven seasons saw Robinson earn an All-Star bid, including in 1991 when he was the league leader in rebounds, and in 1992 when he led the league in blocks per game. His best season came in 1994 when he and Shaquille O'Neal went head-to-head for the NBA scoring title. Robinson needed a massive point total to win the title, and he scored a career-high of 71 points to win the scoring title.

The 1997 season saw Robinson miss the majority of the year with injuries, but it paved the way for the Spurs to draft his predecessor, Tim Duncan. With those two leading the way, the Spurs won two NBA Championships (1999 and 2003). A 10-time All-Star, Robinson, was also named the best defender in the league in 1994, and was said to be one of the best players not only in the history of Spurs but also in NBA history.

Dennis Rodman

Dennis Rodman is known as the most colorful and maybe the most misunderstood player in league history. He was a fantastic defender and rebounder who knew his role better than anyone else. He joined the Detroit Pistons after the 1986 NBA Draft, joining the team with the nickname "Bad Boys." As a rough and rugged group, Rodman fit right in during his first three seasons due to his style of play. Coming off the bench, he provided rebounding, defense, and flat-out effort.

With Rodman playing more in the 1990 season, he was able to secure his first NBA Defensive Player of the Year award, a feat he achieved one more time in his career. His Piston's team won the NBA titles back-to-back in 1989-1990 but had little success in his final seasons with the team. A trade to San Antonio put Rodman in the graces of David Robinson.

His time at Spurs went unsteady as Rodman began to show his colorful side. He dyed his hair a variety of shades, and often clashed and fought with players, coaches, referees, and front-office personnel. Prior to the 1996 season, the Bulls traded for Rodman, and they won three consecutive championships, 1996-1998. Rodman played his role, winning the final three of his seven consecutive rebounding titles while providing his All-NBA caliber defense.

While his career fizzled out over the next two seasons, Rodman still remains in the headlines to this day. Most notably, he has formed a relationship with North Korea leader Kim Jong-Un.

Dirk Nowitzki

One of the best foreign-born players in NBA history, Dirk Nowitzki, transformed himself from a wide-eyed European into a German machine. He started his playing career in the German club, DJK Wurzburg, in the second tier of the German Bundesliga. In 1998, Nowitzki chose not to play in college and was instead selected by Milwaukee in the 1998 draft, where he was traded to Dallas that same night.

In the first couple of seasons in Dallas, Nowitzki struggled with his game, and the team did not reach the playoffs. However, during his third season, Dirk and the Mavericks won 53 games and made the playoffs. This was the first of 12 straight seasons Dirk led his team to the playoffs.

During that run, the Mavericks made the NBA Finals twice, winning Nowitzki's only title in 2011. He was also the first European-born player to win the MVP of the league in 2007 after shooting a career-high from the field (50.2%) and averaging 24.6 points, almost nine rebounds, and three assists per game. Once the streak of 12-straight playoff appearances ended, Dirk never played with the Mavericks in the second round of the playoffs for the rest of his career.

With 2019 as his final season, Nowitzki made it memorable; he finished the season with the 6th most points scored in league history and became the highest-scoring player from outside the United States. He was added as a special addition to the All-Star game, his 14th and final time.

Dwyane Wade

One of the best shooting guards to play the game, Dwyane Wade, combined his big-man post moves in his guard-sized body to consistently wreak havoc around the rim. A slasher combined with an uncanny ability to finish through contact brought Wade to superstar heights. When his college playing days at Marquette University were completed, he was picked by the Miami Heat in the 2003 Draft, 5th overall.

The Heat got off to a slow start in Wade's first year, but he picked up his play, and the team finished strong. Due to his performance, Wade was praised along with the rest of the best rookies of the year. In 2006, Wade and the Heat won the NBA Championship. He was then selected as the Finals MVP after averaging almost 35 points per game, becoming the 5th youngest to achieve that feat.

The summer of 2010 turned into one of the most famous summers, as LeBron James and Chris Bosh both joined Wade in Miami to form the "Big Three." With the trio in place, the Heat went to the NBA Finals four consecutive times, winning twice. After James left to go back to Cleveland, Wade only played one more season in Miami before joining his hometown team, Chicago Bulls, for two seasons. A brief stint in Cleveland saw Wade being traded back to Miami in February of 2018.

In 2019, NBA Commissioner Adam Silver specially added Wade to the NBA All-Star game, for the 13th and final time of his career. Dwyane Wade finished his career first in career points and assists in Miami Heat's history.

Giannis Antetokounmpo

Known as "The Greek Freak" (either for his freakish athleticism, or for the fact that his name is hard to pronounce), Giannis Antetokounmpo had just started to scratch the surface of his basketball abilities.

Born in Greece to parents of Nigerian descent, Antetokounmpo played on the Greek National team before being taken as the 15th overall in the 2013 NBA Draft by Milwaukee. During his first few seasons in the league, Antetokounmpo was merely trying to find his way through. As a young Buck, Antetokounmpo made his debut as one of the youngest ever at the age of 18 years, 311 days.

His first three years never blossomed into what fans see now, but he flashed glimmers of dominance; that all changed at the end of the 2016 season. Antetokounmpo filled out his first triple-double and also scored a career-high of 34 points in a single game, all within a space of two months. This consistent dominance showed the Bucks' fans what the future could look like.

Antetokounmpo went four for four in All-Star selections for the next four years, and the Bucks also played in the playoffs every season. The year 2017 brought more awards, as Antetokounmpo was able to secure the Most Improve Player award after increasing all of his stats. The 2019 season was actually his best season. The Bucks were able to reach the conference finals for the first time since the turn of the century, and Antetokounmpo was selected as the Most Valuable Player in the league. He was the third youngest player to achieve that feat.

Isiah Thomas

As a fierce competitor with a flashy playing style, Isiah Thomas was the floor general that everyone loved to play with. Thomas got his start at Indiana University under Bob Knight, where he and the Hoosiers won the 1981 NCAA National Championship. Following the title, Thomas was taken by the Detroit Pistons as the second overall pick in the 1981 NBA Draft, where he spent his entire career.

In his first season, Thomas was able to make the All-Rookie team and was picked for the All-Star game. He achieved this feat for the next 11 years, with his final season being the only one in his career without a selection.

The success of the Pistons began when they reached the NBA Finals in 1988. This was the first of three straight Finals appearances, and even though they did not win, Thomas still showed his grit. A severely sprained ankle in Game 6 of the series did not slow him down, as he scored an NBA record 25 points in the third quarter alone.

The following season, Detroit was able to put together the "Bad Boys," a rough and tough group of players known for their physicality. The team was able to return to the finals that season and the next, winning both times. Thomas was able to secure winning both Most Valuable Player awards (regular season and Finals).

This was the height of the success for the team though, as the Chicago Bulls with Michael Jordan started their dynasty the next year. Thomas has also been a well-known executive and coach at the collegiate and professional levels of his basketball post-career.

James Harden

Two signatures of James Harden: his shot and his beard; those two things have propelled Harden from the third piece in a trio, to a high-scoring machine. Harden's signature offense comes from his favorite moves: the step-back three-pointer and the euro-step layup. With those two moves, he has carved out a career that started with the Oklahoma City Thunder. He was taken 3rd overall in 2009 and mainly came off the bench in his time with the Thunder.

The 2012 season saw the Thunder reach the Finals but were unable to win. Following that season, Harden moved to Houston after he and the Thunder failed to reach a contract extension. During the first season with the Houston Rockets, Harden was selected for the All-Star game, a feat he achieved every season with the team even though his first two seasons did not put the Rockets past the second round of the playoffs.

His 2015 season was his best yet, as Harden was voted second as the Most Valuable Player, with the Rockets winning their division in the regular season and reaching the third round of the playoffs. Even though he turned out to be the league leader in assists the following year, it still didn't help him go higher in the MVP voting as he also finished second again. Though, in the 2018 season, Harden was finally voted as the best player in the league; he averaged over 30 points in each game, and his team made it to the conference finals. The following season, Harden upped his scoring to 36.1 points per game, winning the scoring title by over 8 points per game.

Jason Kidd

Jason Kidd, an all-time playmaker, seemingly took his abilities to the next level every season. He was able to take his passing abilities in combination with his rebounding skills to be one of the best stat-sheet stuffers ever. Kidd was the second selection of the 1994 draft by the Dallas Mavericks.

During his first season, he tied Grant Hill for the best rookie award, and also recorded the most triple-doubles of any first-year player. Despite his individual success, turmoil forced the Mavericks to trade Kidd to the Phoenix Suns during the 1996 season. In his time at Phoenix, Kidd led the league in assists and became an All-Star three times each.

In 2001, the New Jersey Nets traded for Kidd, and his immediate impact was felt. During Kidd's first two seasons, the Nets were able to make it to the finals in both seasons, but sadly, they couldn't calm the victories. Kidd stayed in New Jersey for another four seasons before he was traded back to Dallas. There, he teamed up with superstar Dirk Nowitzki to lead Dallas to the NBA Championship in 2011.

Following Kidd's playing career, he began coaching with the Brooklyn Nets just nine days after retiring from playing. After coaching in Brooklyn, Kidd became the head coach in Milwaukee. After his dismissal from the Bucks, Kidd was later appointed as an assistant with the Los Angeles Lakers, where he still works up to date. During his playing time, Kidd was fourth all-time with 107 triple-doubles, had a 10-time All-Star, and was the league leader in assists five times.

John Stockton

The man with the record of the most all-time assists, John Stockton, who is an American, rose from a west coast nobody to have a career that lasted longer and had more success than anyone could have ever predicted. Stockton gained rise as a collegiate nobody from Gonzaga University into the 1984 draft. With many fans not knowing who he was, there was a stunned silence at the NBA draft room when he was selected as the 16th overall pick by the Utah Jazz.

Stockton later made the Jazz fans come to appreciate him. A rough style of play, along with the unselfishness to find an open teammate, led Stockton to have the reputation of a dirty player while still being a favorable teammate. In his career, Stockton led the league in assists per game. This included the 1990 season when he set a league record with 14.5 assists per game.

When Stockton retired, he had the highest number of assists in a career (15,806), with a majority going to Karl Malone. The duo played over 1400 games together, leading the Jazz to the NBA Finals on two occasions; the only times the franchise has done that. Stockton's nose for the ball also led him to the all-time steals record for a career with 3,265, almost 600 more steals than second place.

During his career, Stockton was a 10-time All-Star, who led the league in steals twice, and was enshrined in the Hall of Fame in 2009. Outside of his gameplay, Stockton was famous for wearing short-shorts when he played, with many referring to the shorts as "Stocktons."

Kareem Abdul-Jabbar

Too many records to recall, too many stories to retell, Kareem Abdul-Jabbar is a living legend in every sense of the phrase. The American basketball god, Abdul-Jabbar, played three seasons at UCLA, losing just twice, and won three national championships. As a highly sought-after player, Abdul-Jabbar was the very first selection in the 1969 Draft, after turning down offers to neither play with the Harlem Globetrotters nor the ABA.

Abdul-Jabbar played in Milwaukee for a total of six seasons, and his magnificent playing earned him numerous awards. He was voted as the best rookie in 1970, and he remained in the All-Star every year. Also notable during his time in Milwaukee, Kareem Abdul-Jabbar was born with the name Ferdinand Lewis Alcindor before officially changing his name after converting to Islam in college.

In 1975, the Los Angeles Lakers acquired Abdul-Jabbar in a trade where he won his fourth MVP in the first season. During the 14 seasons he played for the Lakers, Abdul-Jabbar won five NBA Titles, became a three-time MVP, and also paved the way for the Lakers dynasty.

When he retired, Kareem Abdul-Jabbar became the all-time scoring leader (38,387 points scored), made the most field goals (15,837) and played the most minutes (57,446). Abdul-Jabbar was known for two things on-court: his signature goggles (a result of too many times being scratched in the eye) and his patented "sky-hook" shot that many people deemed impossible to defend.

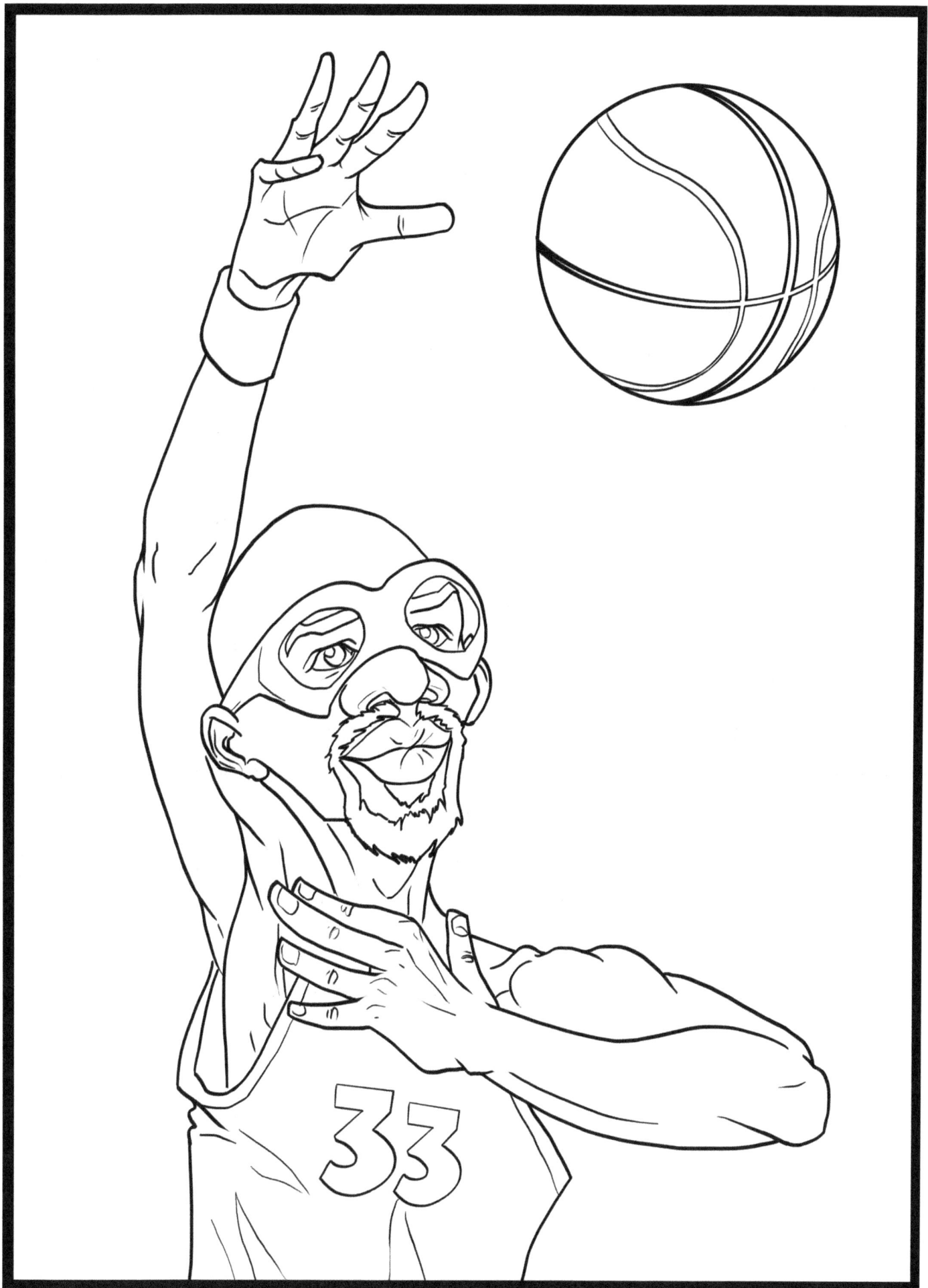

Karl Malone

"The Mailman" Karl Malone, was known as a great power forward and a player who always delivered. Malone was the 13th selection in the 1985 NBA draft who was a relatively unknown commodity in the NBA circles, having grown up near and played at unfamiliar Louisiana Tech University.

Despite reaching the playoffs in the first five seasons, the Jazz only advanced past the first round just once. His individual success came through when he was picked for the first of his 14 consecutive All-Star games, 1988-2001. In the 1989, 1990, and 1992 seasons, Malone finished second in the league in points per game, each time behind Michael Jordan. This was just the beginning, as the most successful portion of his career was coming.

In 1997 and 1998, the Jazz was able to reach the NBA Finals for the first time in franchise history, but they ended up losing both times to the Chicago Bulls. Malone was also voted as the best player in the league in 1997 and again in 1999.

Malone finished his career in 2004 after playing with the Los Angeles Lakers for one season. The Lakers reached the Finals, the third and final time in Malone's career, but he was unable to capture the glory, as the Detroit Pistons ended the championship streak for the 3rd consecutive time for the Lakers. During Karl Malone's career, he was a 14-time All-Star, a two-time MVP, and a Hall of Fame selection in 2010.

Kawhi Leonard

Kawhi Leonard transformed his game from a borderline All-Star to a superstar throughout his career. As a defensive star initially, Leonard earned his nickname, "The Claw," for his abilities to clamp down on any offensive player standing across from him.

After two years at San Diego State University, the Indiana Pacers selected Leonard as the 15th pick in the 2011 Draft and was traded to San Antonio that same night. Leonard was mostly known for his defensive presence than his offensive talent. He allowed the established stars like Tim Duncan, Manu Ginobili, and Tony Parker to flourish offensively.

In 2013, Leonard made his first NBA Finals and averaged 14 points with 11 rebounds per game in the series, but these stats couldn't help his team win the finals. The Spurs finally got their revenge the following year by winning the NBA Finals ahead of the Miami Heat. Kawhi Leonard won the NBA Finals' MVP, mainly for his defense on Heat star, LeBron James.

Leonard ended up making two All-Star teams in his final few seasons with San Antonio, and he was eventually traded to Toronto following the 2018 season. The main reason for the trade stemmed from the difference in opinion on if Leonard had completely recovered from a leg injury he sustained in the 2018 season.

In his only season in Toronto, Kawhi led the Raptors to the NBA Finals, becoming the third player ever to win the Finals' MVP for two different teams. Following that season, Kawhi Leonard moved to Los Angeles and signed with the Clippers.

Kevin Durant

One of the best players of the current generation of players, Kevin Durant, has blended his size and skill to become an unstoppable offensive force. Coming out of the University of Texas, Durant was notably thin for his size. Still, everyone noticed his offensive abilities and was selected by the Seattle SuperSonics (now Oklahoma City Thunder) as the second player in the NBA draft in 2007.

Durant was voted as the best rookie, after averaging over 20 points per game for the season, which made him the third teenager to achieve that feat. The 2010 season was a breakthrough season for Durant as he was voted for his first All-Star game, and he became the youngest player to be the league leader in scoring (30.1 points per game). Two years later, Durant led the Thunder to the Finals. Kevin Durant won the 2014 NBA MVP after leading the league in points per game for the fourth time. His acceptance speech is well-known on the internet, as Durant thanked his mother, through tears for "being the real MVP."

His 2015 season in Oklahoma City was riddled with injuries, and Durant only played 27 games. After losing the conference finals to the Golden State in 2016, Durant signed with the Warriors before the next season, a move that many viewed as him taking the easiest route to a championship. Well, Durant won back-to-back championships in 2017 and 2018 with the Warriors.

He ruptured his Achilles in the 2019 playoffs and later signed with the Brooklyn Nets in the off-season.

Kevin Garnett

Kevin Garnett was a player who played the game of basketball with an unparalleled intensity. This intensity, coupled with his fantastic versatility, led him to a successful career that began straight out of high school. He was picked by the Minnesota Timberwolves in the 1995 NBA Draft. Garnett seemed to restart the trend of players skipping college and going straight to the NBA.

Both Minnesota and Garnett had little success in the first couple of seasons, as the team never made it past the first round in his first seven playoff appearances. Garnett was voted the best player in the league in 2004 after his team went just shy of the NBA Finals.

In July of 2007, the Boston Celtics traded for Garnett in exchange for 7 players, as well as a cash consideration. This deal remains the largest unbalanced trade in league history. In 2008, the Celtics won the league title, and Garnett was voted as the best player of the year.

The final years of his career landed Garnett in Brooklyn for two seasons, and then, he finally returned to Minnesota in 2015. He retired in 2016, expressing his desire to play one more season, but stating that his knees would not hold up for another season. Garnett was a 15-time All-Star (12-straight from 2000-2011), a four-time leading rebounder, and an all-time defender in his time.

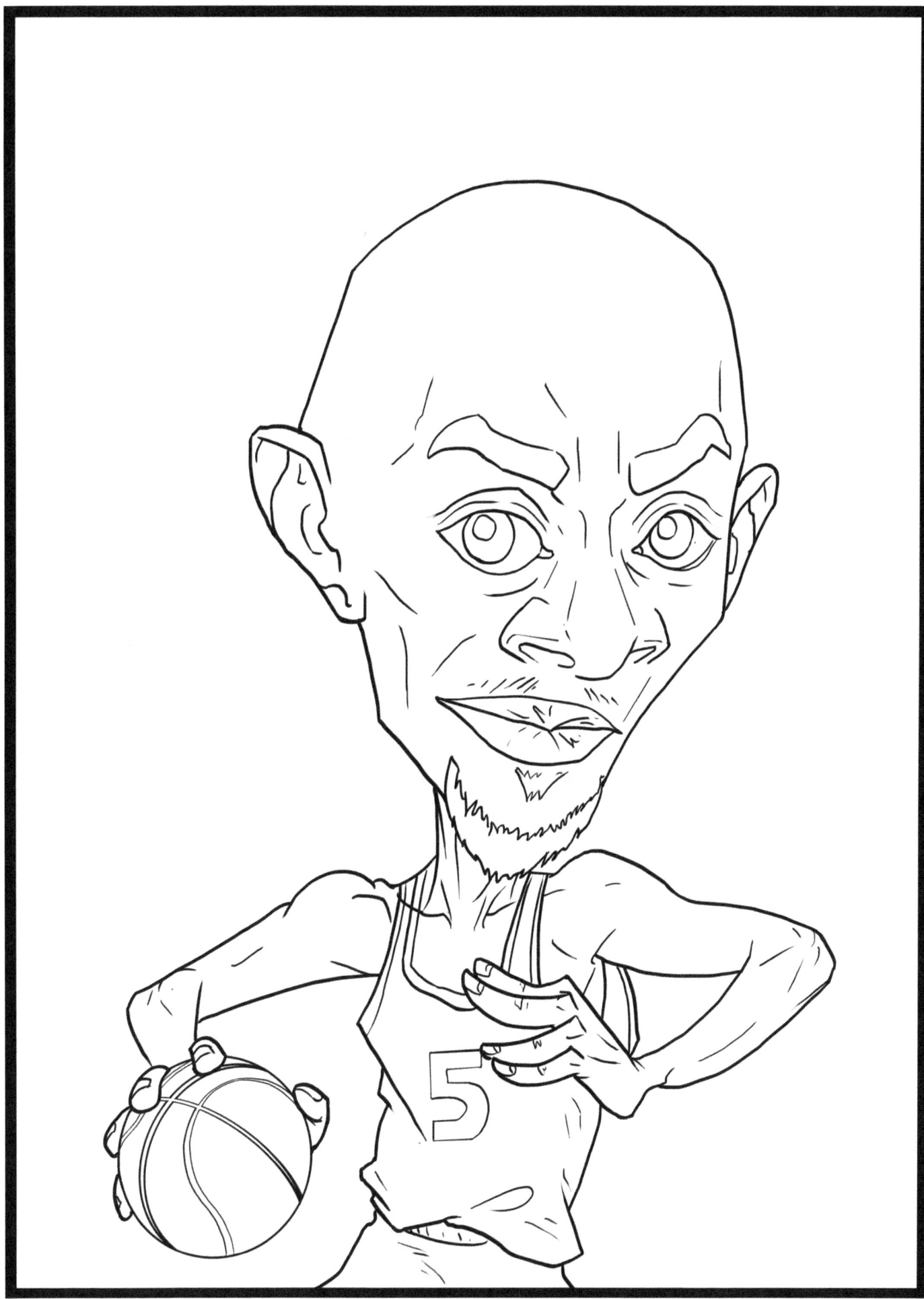

Klay Thompson

A pure shooter to the very definition of the term, Klay Thompson, stars as one part of the "Splash Brothers" duo with the Golden State Warriors. Drafted 11th overall in the 2011 NBA Draft by the Warriors, Thompson immediately made an impact with teammate Stephen Curry (the other half of the "Splash Brothers"). He was placed to the NBA Rookie Team after improving his stats over the length of the season.

In the 2013 season, Thompson and Curry combined to make a-then record of 483 three-pointers, the most by two teammates in a season. The duo went on to break that record the next season. The following season, Thompson was able to increase his career-high for points in a game. In one of those games, Thompson scored 37 points in one quarter, a league record, and all the way to 52 total points in the game. He was also selected to his first All-Star game that year.

The 2016 season saw the Warriors win 73 games, an NBA record, but lost in the Finals. The Warriors went back to the finals the next year and won the 2017 championship. During that year, Thompson scored 60 points in three quarters versus the Indiana Pacers, a game that Thompson dribbled the ball a total of 11 times.

The Warriors won back-to-back titles in 2018, as they defeated the Cleveland Cavilers. The 2019 season ended in the NBA Finals, with Thompson tearing his ACL in game 3 as the Warriors lost to the Toronto Raptors.

Kobe Bryant

Kobe Bryant, the Black Mamba, the fiercest competitor in the game, and the one taken from us before he had a chance to fully make an impact beyond the game of basketball, put everything he had into the game he loved.

Drafted as the 13th overall by the Charlotte Hornets during the 1996 NBA Draft, he was traded that same night to the Los Angeles Lakers, where he spent his entire career. Bryant teamed up with Shaquille O'Neal to bring dominance to LA. The duo went on to win three consecutive titles from 2000-2002, therefore making Kobe the youngest player to win three championships.

The 2003 season was marred with controversy, as Bryant was involved in a sexual assault case during the early part of the season, which forced him to miss out in some games. The Lakers made the Finals for the fourth straight season but lost to the Detroit Pistons. O'Neal was later traded to Miami after years of feuding with Bryant.

In 2006, Bryant scored 81 points during a game in Toronto. It was the second-highest number of points ever scored by one player in a single game in league history. Bryant reached the NBA Finals three more times, from 2008-2010, winning the final two series and also winning the Finals MVP both times. Bryant desperately wanted to match Michael Jordan's six championships during the rest of his career, but he never made it back to the finals. Bryant died during a helicopter crash on January 26, 2020.

Kyrie Irving

Kyrie Irving always seems to have the basketball on his hands like a yo-yo, devastating the defense with his ball-handling abilities. He is also a polarizing figure off the court. Irving was the first pick in the 2011 NBA draft and joined the Cleveland Cavilers.

He was voted the best rookie of the league in 2012, coming up three votes shy of being unanimously selected. In 2015, with LeBron James and Kevin Love in the team, Cleveland reached the Finals, but Irving fractured his kneecap in the first game, and the Cavilers lost the series to the Warriors in 6 games. The Caliver won their championship the next year, as they made history in being the first team ever to come back from a 3-1 deficit in the NBA Finals to win the series. Irving made a three-pointer with less than a minute to play in game seven, to give the Cavilers the lead. The shot was considered one of the most impressive shots in league history because of its importance.

After returning and losing in the 2016 NBA Finals, Boston traded for Irving in July 2016, where he missed the final three months in his first season in Boston due to injuries. In 2019, Irving had a career-high in assists per game, but the Celtics were unable to get past the conference semi-finals. In the off-season, Irving signed with Brooklyn.

Off the court, Irving became famous for dressing up as an old man and playing pickup basketball games at recreational courts, using the name "Uncle Drew." He then went on to star in a movie as that same character.

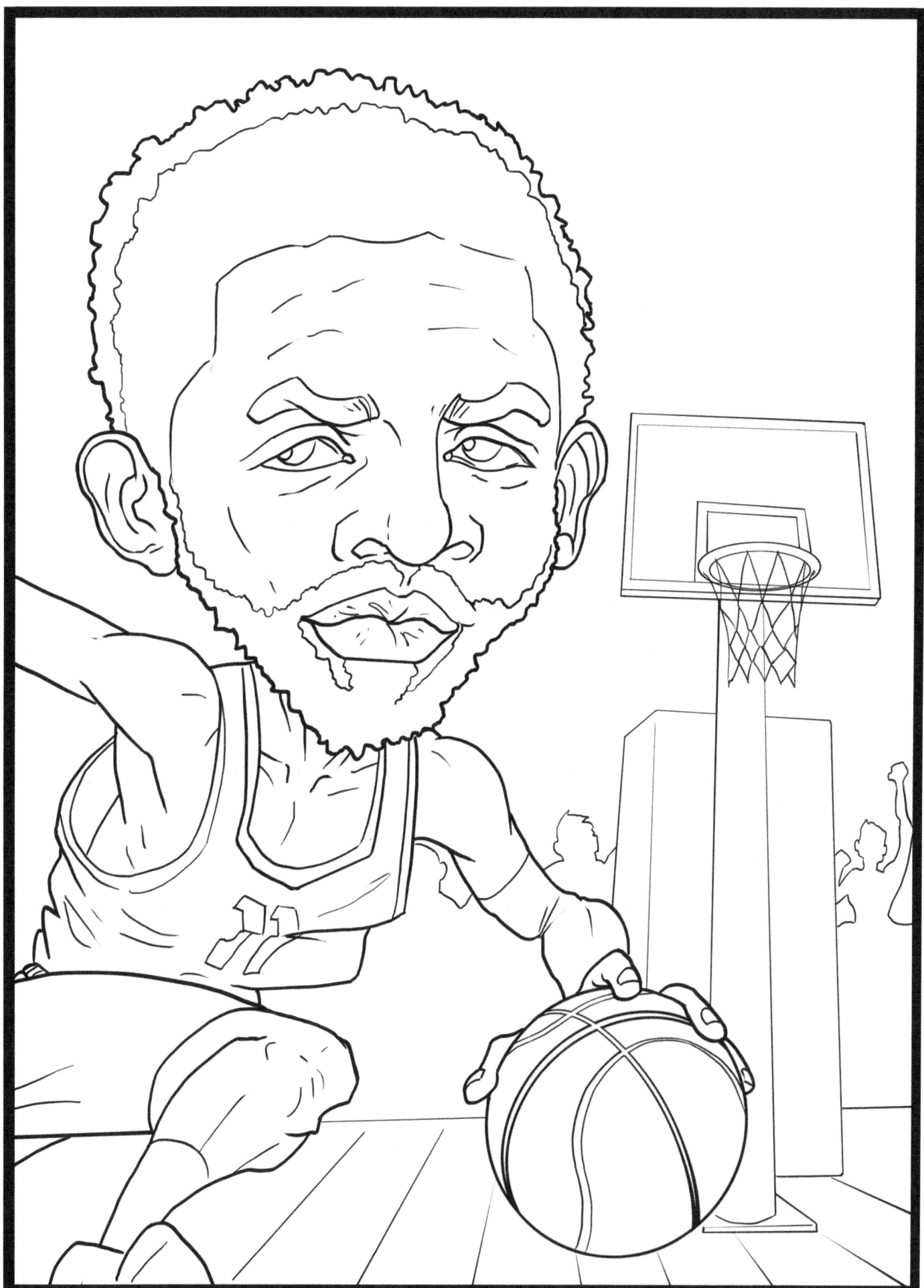

Larry Bird

A pure scorer and an overall great player, Larry Bird, is considered as one of the greatest players ever. While many lauded his playing style, Bird was also a part of one of the greatest rivalries ever, with he and Magic Johnson going head-to-head in numerous championship games.

The first of which came at the collegiate level in 1979, where Bird's Indiana State lost to Johnson's Michigan State. He was the 6th pick in the 1978 draft but only signed with Boston prior to the 1979 draft. Bird was voted as the best rookie in the league in 1980, and his team went on to reach the Eastern Conference Finals.

Bird won his first championship in 1981 but missed reaching the finals in the next two seasons. The year 1984 was the award year for Bird, as he won the triple crown (regular season MVP, Finals MVP, and the NBA Championship). It was just the beginning as Bird went on to win two more MVPs in a row, becoming the third player ever to win three straight MVPs.

The 1987 season was the last time Larry Bird appeared in the Finals, as the Celtics lost to Johnson's Lakers. His final seasons in Boston were cut short due to injuries that ultimately led to his retirement.

Larry Bird's post-playing career was also a success, as he went on to achieve greatness in other aspects of the game. He also won both the Coach of the Year (2000) and Executive of the Year (2012) with the Indiana Pacers.

LeBron James

LeBron James is arguably the greatest player ever and has remained a household name since his high school days in Northeast Ohio. He started his career with the Cleveland Cavilers, winning the Rookie of the Year award.

His extraordinary talent, as well as his immediate rise to stardom, made him noticed around the league, which led him to be picked for the All-Star game in 2004. Two seasons later, LeBron took another step up in his play, being voted second on the MVP ballot and leading his team to the playoffs. In 2007, LeBron led the Cavilers to the NBA Finals despite the team not having any other star aside him. A couple of years later, James won the league MVP, the first of two in a row for him.

After the 2010 season, during a televised broadcast named "The Decision," James announced that he was joining the Miami Heat. In his four seasons in Miami, the team advanced to the finals all four seasons, winning back-to-back titles in 2012-13 with James winning both regular season and finals MVP in both years.

After losing the finals in 2014, James signed back with Cleveland in the offseason, in his quest to bring a championship to his home-state team. In the three seasons he played in Cleveland, LeBron led the Cavilers to three consecutive finals, with the 2016 championship ending Cleveland's 50-year championship drought. The Los Angeles Lakers then went on to sign James in June of 2018.

Magic Johnson

An excellent passer and a person who made the best of their situation, Earvin "Magic" Johnson, lived up to the billing as someone who made magic out of nothing on and off the court.

As the first overall selection by Los Angeles in the 1979 NBA Draft, Magic Johnson made his presence felt immediately, leading his team to the NBA Finals in 1980. With Kareem Abdul-Jabbar injured and not playing in game six, Johnson played just about every position on the court on the way to a dominant performance and winning the finals MVP.

He won his second championship and finals MVP in 1982 with Pat Riley taking over as head coach during the season. The Lakers also reached the finals in 1983 and 1984 but lost both finals with Johnson calling the 1984 loss, the one that got away. Johnson was able to regain the title in 1985 and 1987, winning the regular season's MVP and the NBA Finals MVP that year. The final championship came a year later, with Johnson and the Lakers repeating their victory in 1988.

The final part of his career was marred by controversy. Before the 1991-92 season, Johnson learned he was HIV-positive after a physical. He abruptly retired and did not play for four seasons, in the exception of the 1992 NBA game, when he was voted as a starter by the fans. Johnson played 32 games in the 1995-96 season before retiring for good.

Outside of basketball, Johnson has been involved as a part-owner of the Lakers, Los Angeles Dodgers, Los Angeles Sparks, and Los Angeles Football Club.

Manu Ginobili

One of the most celebrated foreign players in the NBA, Manu Ginobili, had unparalleled success in European basketball and in the NBA on the way to an unlikely career. Ginobili was a late arrival to the NBA, having played in Italy at the beginning of the century and winning a Euro League Title and MVP in 2001.

Drafted in 1999, Ginobili did not sign with the Spurs until 2002. The Spurs advanced to the Finals the next season, with Ginobili providing an unsuspected spark off the bench, forcing opponents to focus on another offensive weapon for the superior Spurs. The Spurs won the 2003 Finals, which led Ginobili to secure more playing time in the following seasons.

His first All-Star selection came in 2005, as the Spurs once again won the championship. Ginobili was close to winning the Finals MVP, as he upped his points per game (20.8) and rebounds per game (5.8) in the series. In 2007, Ginobili started to come off the bench more to provide a spark, and the ploy worked as he won his 3rd championship with the Spurs. In 2008, Ginobili was named the 6th Man of the Year as he increased his points, assists, and rebounds per game, along with his three-point percentage.

2013 was the next time Ginobili and the Spurs appeared in the Finals, thereby losing to the Miami. The Spurs won Ginobili's fourth and final championship the following year after getting their revenge against the Heat. In 2018, Manu Ginobili retired from the San Antonio Spurs and the league.

Michael Jordan

The GOAT, or Greatest Of All Time, Michael Jordan, is the pinnacle of basketball glory and the player everyone is going to be compared to. He starred in college at the University of North Carolina-Chapel Hill, where his rise to fame there was scoring the game-winning basket in the 1982 National Championship game. The Chicago Bulls selected him as the 3rd pick in the 1984 Draft, and Jordan went on to be voted the best rookie in the league for the 1985 season.

The year 1987 became the breakout year for Jordan, as he led the league in scoring (35 points per game). He was also voted as the best defensive player in the league, and he also led the Bulls into the second round of the playoffs.

The first of three-peat began in 1991 as Jordan was named MVP for the second time and led the Bulls through the playoffs, only losing twice. The Bulls went on to win the next two titles, establishing a dynasty.

That ended after 1993, as Jordan retired and signed a minor league contract with the Chicago White Sox of Major League Baseball. For one season, Jordan played with the Birmingham Barons but came back to the Bulls midway through the 1995 season.

The Bulls went on to win three championships in a row from 1996-1998. Jordan won all six Finals MVPs, an NBA record, and retired for the second time in January of 1999 and later returned to play two more seasons with the Washington Wizards from 2001-2003. Jordan was a 14-time All-Star, 5-time MVP, 10-time scoring champion, the 1985 Rookie of the Year, and considered the greatest player of all time.

Patrick Ewing

An all-time favorite player at both the collegiate and professional level, Patrick Ewing, earned recognition starting at Georgetown University. He appeared in the national championship game three times in four years.

After college, Ewing was selected first by the New York Knicks in the 1985 draft. He was the best rookie in the league, despite missing more than 30 games due to injuries. In the 1992 playoffs, Ewing had his iconic game, as he played with a severely sprained ankle to score 27 points to win the game.

Ewing led the Knicks to two championship appearances, once in 1994 with Michael Jordan out of the league, and the other in 1999. The year 1999 was special because the Knicks entered the playoffs as the 8th seed (out of 8) in the Eastern Conference and defeated the entire higher-seeded teams to play in the Finals. Ewing never won a championship, a result of having to play in the same era as Jordan and the Bulls. He finished his career playing two more seasons, one in Seattle and the other in Orlando.

After his playing career, Ewing went on to become an assistant coach at numerous stops in the NBA. He was hired back at his Alma Matter, Georgetown, in 2017 and has been their head coach for the past three seasons.

Paul Pierce

An elite offensive player, Paul Pierce, is known as "The Truth" for his ability to match any opponent offensively and lead his team. Pierce had a relatively good collegiate career, a notable player in his conference, and was picked as the 10th overall pick in the 1998 NBA Draft by Boston.

He had initial success in the NBA, both individual and with the Celtics. Nonetheless, Pierce was unable to win a league title in his first nine seasons. It was in the 2008 season when the Celtics acquired two All-Stars, Ray Allen and Kevin Garnett, that Boston saw a championship. In the 2008 NBA Finals game one, Pierce was injured in the first quarter and was taken off the court in a wheelchair. He returned later in the game, leading the Celtics to the championship and also winning the MVP of the Finals.

Pierce's Celtics returned to the finals a few years later in 2010 but lost to the Lakers. Pierce played with the Celtics through 2013 but was traded to Brooklyn a day before the 2013 NBA draft.

During his two seasons in Brooklyn, the Nets were never able to succeed like they were supposed to. The team never reached the Eastern Conference Finals. Pierce next played in Washington, D.C. for one year and then finished his career in Los Angeles with the Clippers.

Pierce almost had his career derailed in 2001 when he was attacked and stabbed 11 times in his face/neck area. He was carried by a teammate to a nearby hospital where he underwent surgery.

Reggie Miller

One of the greatest outside shooters in league history, Reggie Miller, gained a reputation as a player willing to put everything on the line to take down his opponents. The Indiana Pacers picked Miller as the 11th overall in the 1987 NBA Draft. The fans of the Pacers, who desperately wanted a local player from Indiana University to be selected, did not welcome Miller initially.

His early career saw him rise from a bench player to a starter and formidable scorer. He had a few iconic moments in the mid-1990s playoffs: in the 1994 Eastern Conference Finals, Miller scored 39 points, 25 in the fourth quarter alone, to lead an upset victory over the Knicks in New York. Perhaps his greatest feat came a year later, also against the Knicks. In the Eastern Conference semi-finals, the Pacers trailed the Knicks by six points, and Miller went on to score eight points in the next nine seconds to stun the Knicks, which gave the Pacers the win.

In 2000, the Pacers reached the Finals for the first and only time but lost. It was the only finals appearance in Miller's and the Pacer's franchise history. When he retired, Miller was the leader in career three-point shots made with over 2,500, a record that has been broken. He was inducted into the NBA Hall of Fame in 2012. Reggie Miller now works as a television analyst for TNT.

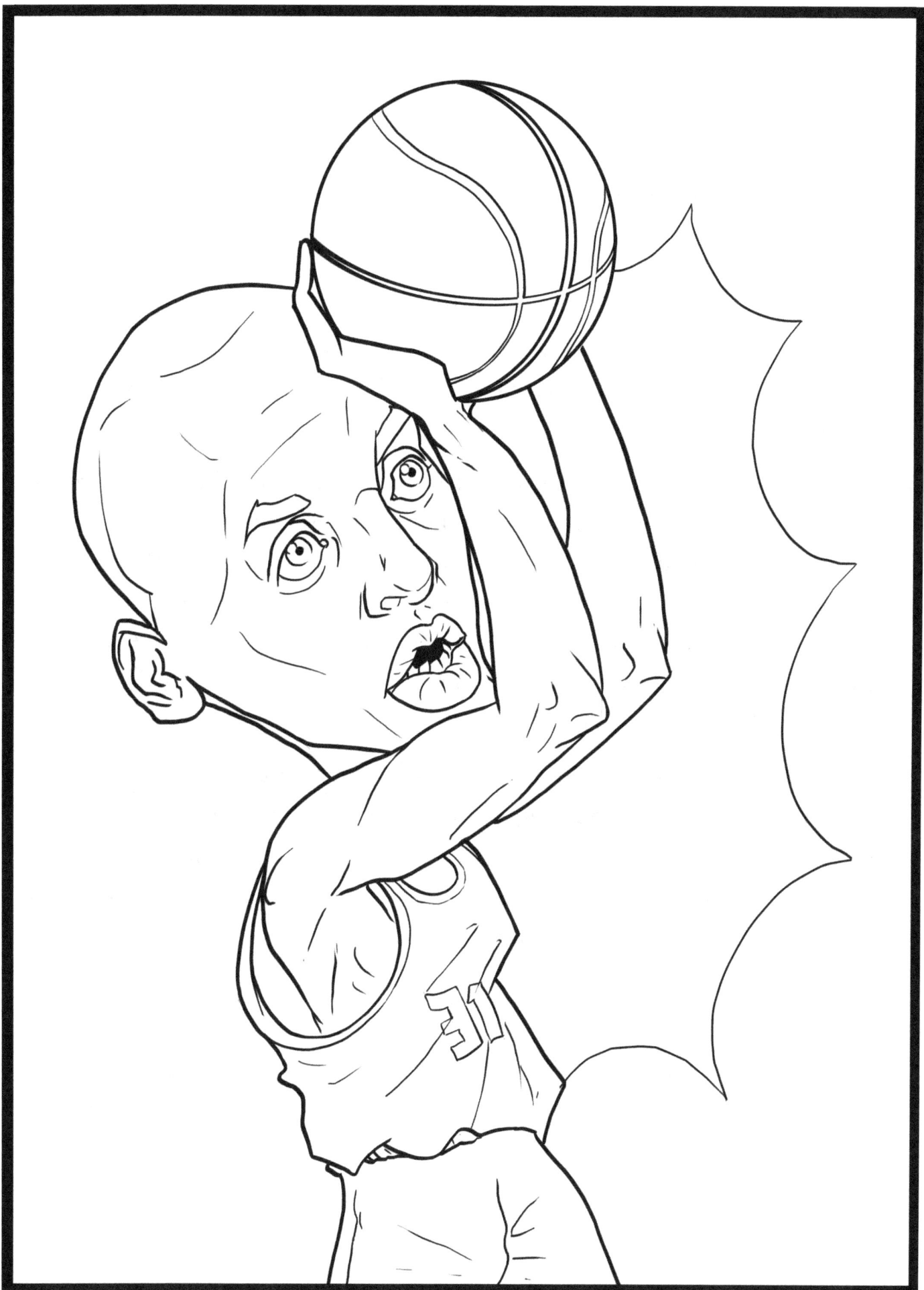

Russell Westbrook

A freak of nature and infinitely intense, Russell Westbrook, has turned his athletic advantage into a career of stuffing stat sheets. Westbrook joined the NBA after a fantastic collegiate career with the Bruins of the University of California at Los Angeles.

He was selected fourth overall by the Seattle Supersonics, who moved and became the Oklahoma City Thunder soon after. In his third season, Westbrook was able to reach the playoffs. In that same season, he was selected to his first All-Star game as well. In the 2012 season, Westbrook's Thunder made history and reached the NBA Finals, the first time in franchise history, but unfortunately, they lost. In 2014, Westbrook missed numerous games as he suffered multiple injuries. This was his only season in the last 10 seasons, where he did not make it to the All-Star game.

His stat-stuffing season in 2017 included averaging a triple-double for a season, becoming the second player to average a triple-double in a season, and it led him to be named as the NBA MVP. In that season, Westbrook also set the record for triple-doubles in a season with 42. This was the beginning of three consecutive seasons that Westbrook went on to average a triple-double in.

In July of 2019, the Houston Rockets traded for Westbrook and teamed him up with former Thunder star, James Harden. In January of 2020, Westbrook had over 19,000 points, 6,000 rebounds, and 7,000 assists in his career, and he remains one of three players to achieve that feat. He is also the second all-time in career triple-doubles with 146.

Scottie Pippen

The Robin to Michael Jordan's Batman, Scottie Pippen, is a great small forward but perhaps an even better teammate and player who knew his role. Having played at NAIA University of Central Arkansas, Pippen gained NBA attraction after he grew seven inches in college and dominated at the NAIA level.

Pippen was selected 5th overall by the Seattle Supersonics but was traded to the Chicago Bulls on that same night. During his first years in the league, Pippen was a role player, who earned his playing time through his defensive play and his versatility on offense. Michael Jordan became a great mentor for Pippen as they played alongside each other, and they both helped each other improve their games.

Pippen and the Bulls went on to win three straight championships from 1991-1993. When Jordan left the Bulls after the 1993 season, Pippen stepped up to become the leader of the team for the year and a half Jordan was gone. When Jordan came back to basketball, the Bulls then went on to win the 1996, 1997, and 1998 NBA Championships, their second three-peat.

The Houston Rockets traded for him prior to the 1998 season. After just one year at the Houston Rockets, he moved to the Portland Trail Blazers, where he played for four seasons. He then signed back with the Bulls in 2003 and played his final season, though his team did not reach the playoffs; this was the first time in his 17-year career. Pippen was a 7-time All-Star and a 10-time All-Defensive team player, leading many to consider him as one of the all-time best defenders.

Shaquille O'Neal

Affectionately known as Shaq, Shaquille O'Neal is a rare unicorn in a league full of talents that changed the game in more ways than one could ever imagine. Shaq was the first selection of the 1992 NBA Draft by Orlando, after playing collegiately at Louisiana State University.

He proved himself quickly in 1993 by winning the Rookie of the Year. His dominance as a center in the league continued as he led the Orlando Magic to the NBA Finals in 1995. He signed with the Los Angeles Lakers and won three consecutive finals along with the finals MVP from 2000-2002, as he teamed up with Kobe Bryant. Shaq also won the regular season's MVP award in the 2000 season. After losing in the 2003 Finals, Shaq played with the Lakers for one more season before being traded to the Miami Heat following rumors of a feud with Kobe.

In Miami, he teamed up with Dwyane Wade to win the 2006 NBA Championship. After three-plus seasons in Miami, he bounded around the league, playing in Phoenix, Cleveland, and finally, Boston.

Known for his big size and personality, Shaq was a lovable character on and off the court. His size caused issues for everyone; the NBA was forced to change their backboards because Shaq broke so many early in his career. He was also the focal point of a tactic known as "Hack-a-Shaq," where teams would purposely foul him because he was such a poor free throw shooter (career 52.7%).

Stephen Curry

The rise of Stephen Curry is unlike most players we have seen in the NBA. A slight shooter, whose best value is extending the defense beyond their stretching point. Curry has taken on a career and life no one saw coming as he first came into limelight from his time at Davidson College, where he led the school to big-time upsets in the NCAA Tournament in 2007 and 2008.

Curry was selected as the 7th pick by the Golden State Warriors in the 2008 NBA Draft and was voted the second-best rookie of the league that year. Curry's beginnings in the NBA were filled with injuries, and in his first four seasons, he missed almost a total of 65 games.

With the drafting of Klay Thompson, the duo became known as the "Splash Brothers," and Curry set the league record for three-pointer field goals made in a single season in 2013. Curry won the MVP Award despite sitting out numerous fourth quarters with his team winning the games by so many points, and his team won the Finals. His most historic season came in 2016 when he was the league leader in points per game and was voted MVP, the first unanimous winner in league history. His Warriors also won an NBA-record of 73 games but lost the Finals.

The Warriors then won the championship in 2017 and 2018 but lost in 2019. At the beginning of the 2019-2020 season, Curry injured his hand and missed over four months of the season. Stephen Curry is considered one of the best shooters in NBA history and has changed the way the game is played.

Steve Nash

One of the best ball-handling guards, Steve Nash, had a knack for being able to work well with big men, and he became one of the best passers during his time of play. Nash was chosen with the 15th pick in the 1996 NBA Draft but did not play for long with the Phoenix Suns.

The Dallas Mavericks traded for Nash in 1998, where he teamed up with Dirk Nowitzki. In 2001, the Mavericks made the playoffs for the first time since 1990. He stayed in Dallas for a few more years and then signed back with the Phoenix Suns.

In 2004, he led the Suns to the league's best record (62 wins). During that season, he became the league leader in assists and won the MVP. He also became the first person born in Canada and the third point guard to win the award. Nash won the MVP the following season, as he set career highs in points, rebounds, field goal percentage, and free-throw percentage while still leading the league in assists. The following season, Nash averaged over 18 points and 11 assists per game, the second player to have those numbers. But he was edged out by former teammate Dirk Nowitzki for the league MVP.

After finishing his time with the Suns, Nash signed with the Los Angeles Lakers in 2012. But injuries derailed his time, and he only played in 65 out of a possible 164 games. Nash officially retired in March of 2015. For his career, Nash was an eight-time All-Star, two-time MVP, and was a league leader in assists five times.

Tim Duncan

"The Big Fundamental," Tim Duncan, was one of the most consistently dominating players of his generation. Swimming was his initial sport, but after the only Olympic-sized pool on his native U.S. Virgin Islands was destroyed in a hurricane, in his freshman year of high school, Duncan took up basketball.

For four years, he played at Wake Forest University and was named the player of the year in the NCAA in his final season. The San Antonio Spurs picked him first overall in the 1997 NBA Draft, where he teamed up with future Hall of Famer David Robinson and became the best rookie in the league that year.

The 1999 season brought Duncan his first championship, as he and Robinson dominated the series with Duncan winning the Finals MVP. Duncan's best year came in 2002 when he posted career highs in points, rebounds, assists, and blocks on the way to the league MVP. He bested his rebounding stats the next year and won back-to-back MVPs as the Spurs won the NBA Championship with Duncan winning the Finals MVP.

2005 and 2007 brought two more championships, with Duncan winning Finals MVP in the 2005 series. His fifth and final championship came in 2014, as he became the second player ever to win a championship in three different decades. Duncan finished out his career with the Spurs, retiring in 2016. In July of 2019, Spurs added Tim Duncan as one of their assistant coaches.

Tony Parker

Though he was slight in stature, Tony Parker, a French-American, was a creative guard who was able to find ways to make plays, and this made him become a huge part of multiple championship teams. After having played professionally for two years in France, Parker was picked as the 28th selection by the San Antonio Spurs in the 2001 NBA draft. At the end of his first season, Parker had gone from a bench player to leading the Spurs in assists and steals. He became the first player born outside the United States to be selected to the All-Rookie team.

2003 was the first championship for Parker, but he was benched numerous times for more veteran guards late in games. The second championship came two years later, with Parker again struggling in the Finals and having to have others take over the guard position. Following his impressive display in the next season, Parker was selected as an All-Star for the very first time.

In 2007, the Spurs went back to the Finals, and this time Parker dominated. He led his team in scoring in the series and won the Finals MVP, becoming the first foreign-born player to win the award. The Spurs also reached the Finals two more times, losing in 2013 but winning Parker's fourth championship in 2014.

Parker finished his career after playing one season in Charlotte before retiring in 2019. For his career, Parker was a six-time All-Star, four-time NBA Champion, and considered one of the best guards born outside the U.S. to play in the NBA.

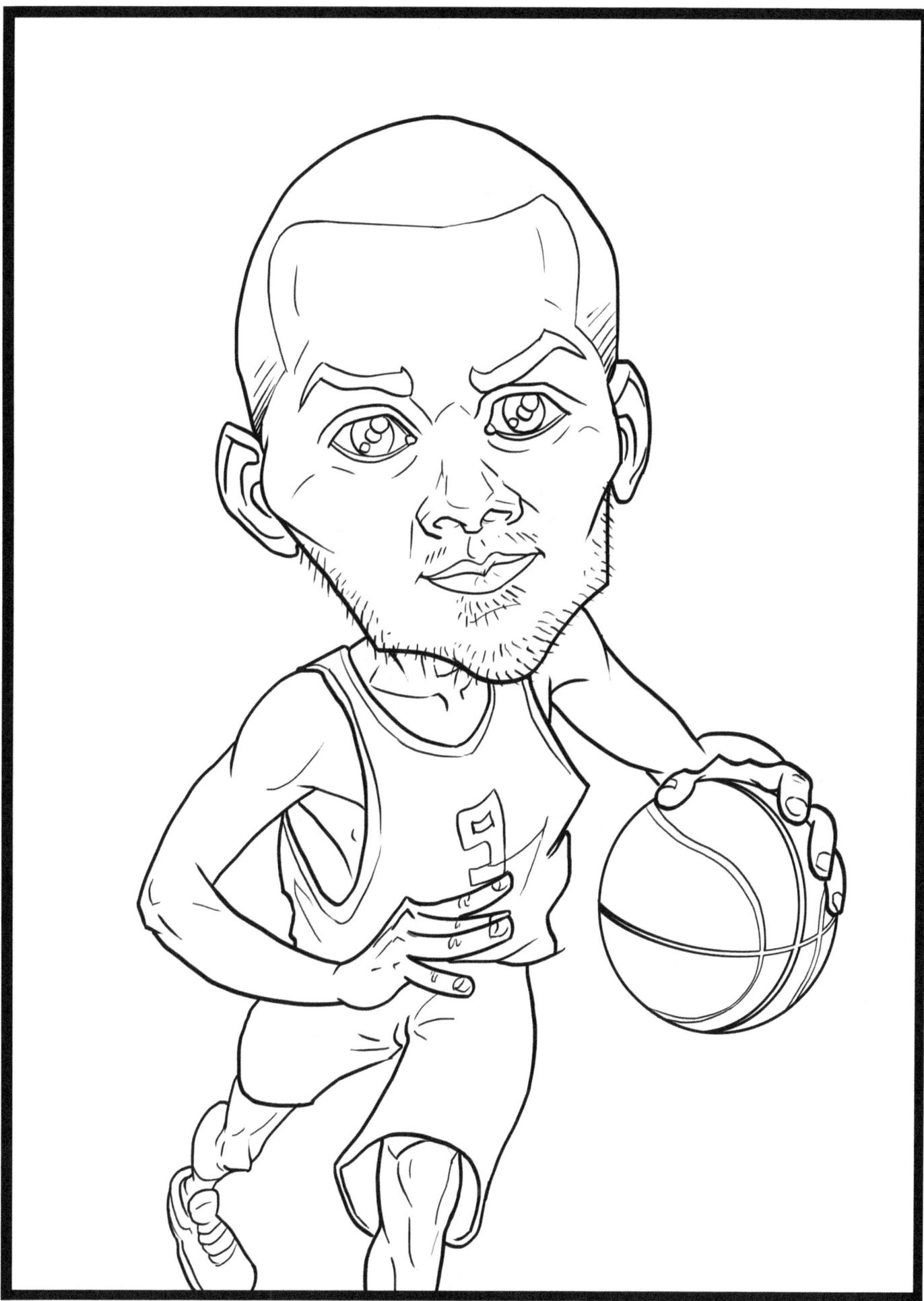

Vince Carter

Vince Carter is a high-flyer who was dubbed "Half-Man/Half-Amazing." He was a player whose career spanned longer than most would have thought, considering his playing style. Carter began his career with the Toronto Raptors after being traded by Golden State, who took him 5th in the 1998 NBA Draft.

Carter won the 1999 Rookie of the Year and began his career as a high-flyer who wowed fans with his dunks. Notably, Carter won the 2000 Dunk Contest, a contest that still resonates with fans to this day.

In December of 2004, the New Jersey Nets traded for Carter. During his first season with the Nets, he increased his points per game average by over 11 points versus his time in Toronto during that same season. While in New Jersey, Carter saw success, but they didn't advance past the conference semi-finals. Carter made his only conference finals in 2010 with the Orlando Magic after being traded to the team. The Phoenix Suns, Memphis Grizzlies, Dallas Mavericks, Sacramento Kings, and the Atlanta Hawks are all teams Carter has also played for in his 24-year career.

Vince Carter is the only player in NBA history to play in four different decades (1990s, 2000s, 2010s, 2020s), a feat that did not seem possible with his playing style, as well as the injuries he sustained in the early days of his playing career. Carter is most known for his dunking abilities, with perhaps his most infamous one coming in the 2000 Olympics when he dunked over 7'2" French Center, Frederic Weis.

Yao Ming

The most famous big man to play in the modern NBA, Yao Ming, made a large impact on the court in the little time he played in the game. Yao is a Chinese-American who began his playing career in China with the Shanghai Sharks junior team. After four years, Yao was moved up to the senior Sharks roster, where he led the team to three consecutive Chinese Basketball Association Championship games during his last three seasons, winning the final year.

Initially, Yao had trouble getting permission from the Chinese government to let him play basketball in America. Finally, the Chinese government granted his request, and the Houston Rockets selected Yao as the first overall in the 2002 draft. He was voted as the second-best rookie of the league but was later voted as an All-Star in 2003.

As accomplished as Yao became on the court, his size proved to be his downfall as injuries began to mount up starting in 2005. He played in five more seasons, but the most games he played in the 2009 season was 77. Yao missed the entire 2010 season due to a foot injury and played only five games in the next season before retiring in 2011.

Yao's biggest impact might be his ability to bridge the gap between the NBA and the basketball-hungry fans in China. During a game in the 2007 season, Yao played Yi Jianlian, a fellow Chinese basketball professional, in an NBA game. Over 200 million fans in China watched the game, which made the game one of the most viewed games in league history.

Allen Iverson

Pound for pound, possibly the greatest little man to ever play the game, Allen Iverson did more with less than any other player. Listed at a generous 6'0", 165 pounds, Iverson's athleticism led him to be named the Virginia Player of the Year in football and basketball.

After graduating, he played two seasons at Georgetown University, where he was voted as the best defensive player in the conference in both seasons. He also set the school record for points per game in his career (22.9). He declared for the 1996 NBA Draft and was taken first overall by the Philadelphia 76ers.

Known for his tenacity and ability to get buckets despite his stature, Iverson was a four-time scoring champ, with his career scoring average of 26.7 points per game ranking 9th all-time. His post-season scoring average of 29.7 points per game is the second all-time to the great Michael Jordan. Over his career, Iverson was an 11-time All-Star. He also won the 2001 NBA MVP and was entered into the NBA Hall of Fame in 2016.

Other than his works on the floor, Iverson had his impact felt in so many other fashions. With the rise of hip-hop during his heyday, Iverson brought the flair and fashion of the rap game to his pre-game and post-game interviews and walkthroughs. Cornrows, tattoos, gold chains, and baggy clothes were all parts of his persona, and it brought the two cultures together.

Anthony Davis

Known simply as "The Brow," Anthony Davis was a bona fide superstar before his name was called on the draft night. His rise to fame came in as early as his only season at the college level at the University of Kentucky. Davis grew almost a foot from his freshman year of high school to his senior year, and that allowed him to gain a lot of attention from college coaches. Davis entered his freshman season at Kentucky with enormous expectations following his great rise.

He lived up to those expectations and averaged a double-double while setting the conference and NCAA freshman record by blocking the most shots in a single season. After his retirement, Davis was voted the best freshman, the best defender, and the overall best player in the nation. He also went on to win the national title.

The New Orleans Hornets (now Pelicans) selected Anthony Davis as the first in the 2012 NBA Draft. He was voted second in the Rookie of the Year even though his season ended shorter than expected due to injuries. Over the next six seasons in New Orleans, Davis led the Pelicans to the playoffs twice, where he was also named an All-Star in each season. Davis' extraordinary talent also made him set franchise records for points in a game (59), as well as career points (11,059). In 2019, the Los Angeles Lakers traded for Davis, where he was picked for the All-Star Game for the 7th time.

Ben Wallace

Ben Wallace is perhaps the greatest defensive player of his generation, and he's also the epitome of the phrase "rise from nothing." Wallace is an American retired basketballer that started his collegiate career at Cuyahoga Community College, where for two seasons, he was a defensive menace at the Junior College level. After two more seasons at the DII level with Virginia Union, he went undrafted and had a tryout with an Italian club. Wallace turned a Summer League tryout into a spot on the Washington Bullets roster in 1996.

The next five seasons saw him bounced around three different teams before he landed with Detroit. He was second in the league in grabbing rebounds (over 13 per game). Ben Wallace led the league in blocks once in the five seasons he stayed in Detroit, as well as leading the league in rebounding twice. He was also a four-time All-Star and was named the best defender in the league four times.

He also led Detroit to the NBA Finals twice and reached the playoffs in the other two seasons. In the 2004 NBA Finals, the Pistons put a stop to the Los Angeles Lakers dynasty, beating the three-time defending champs. The Pistons went back to the Finals the next season but were unable to repeat their victory, as the San Antonio Spurs won in seven games. Even though Wallace had such an impressive career, it was almost marred by the "Malice at the Palace." The infamous fight between Detroit and Indiana involved players going into the stands to fight fans, and this left Wallace with a six-game suspension.

Blake Griffin

Known for his high-flying dunks, including one over an actual car, Blake Griffin, an American, has made a career and name for himself by being one of the most superior athletes on the court. He starred at the University of Oklahoma, where he was voted as the best player of the year after averaging 23 points and 14 rebounds per game.

He was the first pick of the 2009 draft, but he never played in the opening season. During a preseason game, he landed awkwardly during a dunk attempt and missed the entire season with the Los Angeles Clippers due to injury. His official rookie season was in 2010, and it ended up being an all-time great first season. He led all rookies in scoring (22.5 points per game) and rebounding (12.1 per game). He was voted as the best rookie, becoming the first player since 1990 to be voted unanimously.

The next four seasons for Griffin landed him in the All-Star game and the playoffs each time. From 2015-2018, however, Griffin missed over 100 games due to a variety of injuries. In January of 2018, the Detroit Pistons traded for Griffin, and he finished that season with Detroit, but his points and rebounds per game were at an all-time low. He turned it around the following season, where he was named to his 6th All-Star game and averaged a career-high with 24.5 points per game.

THANK YOU!

Have questions? We want to hear from you!
Email us at: support@activitywizo.com

Please consider writing a review!
Just visit: activitywizo.com/review

www.ingramcontent.com/pod-product-compliance
Lightning Source LLC
Chambersburg PA
CBHW081754100526
44592CB00015B/2436